بستانِ خیال

The Walled Garden of Enchantment

A Recapturing of Siraj Aurangabadi's
Bustan-e-Khayal in English

AC Benus

an AC Benus Impression
San Francisco

Grateful acknowledgement is here offered
for the support and encouragement
I've received on the literary site
www.gayauthors.org.

ISBN 978-1-953389-44-2 (ebook)
ISBN 978-1-953389-43-5 (paperback)

Cover photo: pxfuel.com

Vignettes:
From author's 1910 edition of *The Grammar of Ornament*

Poetry Available from AC Benus

Hymenaios, or The Marriage of the God of Marriage
A Classical style myth in 2,600 lines of Blank Verse
ebook: ISBN 9781953389091; paperback: ISBN 9781953389084

Summer 2020 – Hell in a Handbasket
A contender for the Pulitzer Prize in poetry, 2021, this collection grapples with the year of pandemic, racial injustice and environmental crisis
ebook: ISBN 9781953389015; paperback: ISBN 9781953389008

The Thousandth Regiment
A Translation of and Commentary on Hans Ehrenbaum-Degele's First World War Poems "Das tausendste Regiment"
ebook: ISBN 1657220583; paperback: ISBN 9781657220584

A Man in a Room, and other poems
Verse following the year when the poet was 21 years old
ebook: ISBN 97817345103; paperback: ISBN 978173456107

The Easiest Thing in the World, and other poems
Marking the third anniversary of the Pulse Nightclub terror attack
ebook: ISBN 9781734561029; paperback: ISBN 9781734561036

Rima Fragmenta, or Fragments of a Rift
Fifty Sonnet for Kevin
ebook: ISBN 9781734561005; paperback: ISBN 9781734561012

First Love: Poems for Ross
For everyone's first love; both bitter and sweet
ebook: ISBN 9781734561081; paperback: ISBN 9781734561098

Poetry Available from AC Benus

Demon Dream
Redemption and shared humanity shine in this retelling of a
medieval Japanese legend
ebook: ISBN 9781953389138; paperback: ISBN 9781953389145

Audre Lorde Knows What I Mean – 2021 in Review
A follow-up to Summer 2020, this collection grapples with the
year of the Gop-led Capitol insurrection, racial injustice and the
death throes of the environment
ebook: ISBN 9781953389015; paperback: ISBN 9781953389008

Mikhail Kraminsky, and other poems
Two collections of early poems exploring the pain of youth and
being closeted
ebook: ISBN 9781953389152; paperback: ISBN 9781953389169

One Hundred and Fifty-Five Sonnets for Tony
A bold testament to love
ebook: ISBN 9781953389114; paperback: ISBN 9781953389107;
hardback: ISBN 9781953389121

Love Looked at Me and Laughed – Poems for Brian
Love is not always easy. Poems to/for/about my first boyfriend
ebook: ISBN 9781953389237; paperback: ISBN 9781953389220
hardback: ISBN 978-1-953389-24-4

Love is Love (Contributor)
Poetry Anthology: In aid of Orlando's Pulse victims and
survivors, Lily G. Blunt, Editor, 2016
ebook: ISBN 153514369X; paperback: ISBN 153514369X

Author's Note

Siraj Aurangabadi was an early 18th century Sufi poet. As a lay clergyman in this branch of Islam, he explored the human-condition in relationship to an all-loving, all-forgiving God. In this, he followed the same writing traditions as Hafiz and Rumi before him. Siraj's many ghazals praising the beauty and transformative power of same-sex love are still sung in India and Pakistan today. [i]

What follows is not a "translation" in the proper sense, as the Urdu original of *Bustan-e-Khayal* is inaccessible to me, and even when poets' work in this language are obtainable, the broadness of the poetry – and references to Persian and Arabic predecessors – leaves non-speakers like me at a disadvantage. [ii]

That being said, I am still able to recapture the plot, the couplet formatting, the personal relationships, and the beauty of Siraj's transcendental message about the meaning of earthy love. I have done this by using a detailed summary of the 1738 original. [iii]

Yet above all else, *The Walled Garden of Enchantment* is an exaltation of the love between men which can rise above adversity, such as contrived reasons concerning religious differences, with their ingrained senses of superiority, as well as other societal pressures, like those forcing young men to marry women as part of an expected sacrifice *for the good of the family,* no matter their orientation. In Aurangabadi's work, these compromises are not allowed to happen; the male couples are accommodated – *sans* proselytization or conversion – and accepted in

ways that let their unions stand independently and as equals to cross-sex marriages. In fact, they are celebrated as more important than ordinary, arranged male-female contractual obligations.

Any person who attempts to misrepresent Siraj, and his impressive oeuvre of ghazel lyrics and narrative poetry, as anything but Gay, is willfully trying to perpetrating a hoax. This poet belongs fully to LGBTI2S+ studies and its rich, historic and artistic culture.

And lastly, for those already familiar with the *Bustan-e-Khayal,* or its detailed summary, I must acknowledge adjusting the ending of the original in my version. But must I justify my "recapturing," following an arc of development hinted at in *The Walled Garden of Enchantment,* but remaining unstated?

I feel I have carried the poem out to its logical conclusion, but freely accept that others – presumably those previously captured by the enchantment of Siraj's narrative poetry – will have a bone to pick with me. So be it. [iv]

خبر تحیر عشق سن نہ جنوں رہا نہ پری رہی
نہ تو تو رہا نہ تو میں رہا جو رہی سو بے خبری رہی
—سراج اورنگ آبادی

Listen to the Word of love, for neither apparitions,
Or sprights, nor you or I who stay, will remain unenlightened.
—Siraj Aurangabadi

بستانِ خیال

The Walled Garden of Enchantment

The Walled Garden of Enchantment

Spirits akin to mine, hearken to my fate,
   For all my woes revolve around just one loss.

My heart now no longer bursts forth in parklands,
   Nor finds interest in the towns I must wander. [1]

For no matter offered kingdoms to change course –
   Or the philosopher's stone to make my wealth –

Without my man, head and core are reasonless,
   And the gay world endless despondency finds:

---

[1] A few general points to note from the original text: our ascetic narrator is named Siraj, but this is only mentioned once throughout the entirety of the lengthy poem; he's addressed "Dervish" by his admirers. The protagonist is approximately 28 years of age when telling us his story, and his home city is Hyderabad. The names of the poet's absent partner, and the soldier's son who loves the dervish, are never stated.

He left each breath a spark within my sighing,
   And each chess move a pawn in life's strategy,

For this, dear friends, is how I face each new dawn
   After night has spun her hours of bad dreams —

And yet I feed on the darkness as the light
   Bleeds out my heart every waking beat of day.

So, souls akin to mine, hear this, my sad tale,
   And know each loss is but a loss in the Lord.

Time was, with my rosy-cheeked lover, I felt
   All of life was a divine revelation.

Hand in hand together we'd join drink to talk
   The span of nights ever moonlit and wine-warmed,

For in love's glow, each glance was an embracing
   And every kiss, a *ghazal's* recitation

Where neither word nor song need interfere on
   Quiet acknowledgement of our perfection,

As such moments inevitably led us
   To seek our pillows' private intimacy

Where wills and bodies pure could do just what they
  Wanted to do when out amongst the many.

The *rat-a-tat* of our connectedness still
  Sounding upon eardrums, we'd after treasure

The holding in silence of one another
  Closer, in life overflowing with great joy.

Belovèd beside me, I had no fear of
  What the future could possibly send our way . . . .

But my happily-ever-after was doomed,
  And fairy-tale endings seldom last through life,

Because there are many boys who will render
  Would-be lovers dumbstruck, speechless and blinking.

And it was one such who astray led my mate,
  Sowing false words across gullible beliefs.

For lads like these I would later encounter:
  Boys blessed with allure, but marred by ambition;

The many others who with boundless beauty
  Can display broad Nature's perennial charms;

Young men whose frowns were like springtime blooms of trees;
  Whose glints of eye and youthful strides of motion

Tempted admirers, tricking forth the right
  Stream of words to return in soft enthrallment,

For although their outward visages might make
  Bright mirrors dim and blush in comparison,

And a painter's brush pull out every bristle
  In the frustration of capturing their youth,

The songs of these boys were honey to the depths,
  As the peach fuzz riding their upper lips made

Them enchanting as Yusef or Adonis
  In their thousand faultless, God-granted features.

One like that lured away my belovèd's gaze,
  And later, on my own, such sought me out too,

For the sadness they saw in me enticed them
  More than outspoken courting could ever do.

As an exile, their turbans of brocade silk
  Would approach my desolance respectfully;

Their chests were wreathed in leis of marigold-bright,
    As were their wrists and ankles in the bedroom;

While satin scarves swaddled their throats as neck bands,
    Broader examples encircled slender waists;

Status was shown via dagger and cutlass,
    But each was scabbar'd in gem-set velvet blocks.

Arrayed like this, these alluring gazelles would
    Seduce well-read men with their wiles-couched chatter: [2]

To be loved by the famous was their desire –
    Their way to an assured mention in History.

They knew me as Dervish, one of gentle depth;
    A bittersweet poet singing of heartache;

One leanèd in the ways of Man, but still kind;
    One easy of knowledge, but spare of advice.

And when those kempt boys-on-the-make discovered
    I had students across the breadth of the land

---

[2] With origins in Persian poetic traditions from pre-Muslim times, and with meanings maintained right through to the current day, "gazelle" refers to young men available to other men for relationships.

And that my name was recognized far and wide,
    Around me they gathered with competing charms.

Fawning regard they first applied to soften
    The disinterest perceived in my returned glance.

And when my head failed to linger on them, oh –
    They assumed my sadness an act of coyness.

This they took as goading, saying twix themselves:
    "When we could make lovers of many thousands,

Why should frigid he seem to those who attempt
    To soothe his hurt, to make his nights less lonely

And to give him a new lad to sing about
    Throughout the towns, the farms, and the deserts too?"

Being wise in temptation's Art, they changed tack;
    Replaced student manners with frank seduction.

Regard's distance melted into flirting bold
    As physical separations diminished.

They'd sit themselves next to my reclining form,
    Pausing their lips heart-beat close to mine, trembling.

They'd fenagle their hands to be holding mine
    As a head fell lovingly on my shoulder,

Then use their fingers to run across the hair,
    Or slip slyly between my clothing and skin –

But such poor boys had their digits discover
    Nothing of stiff resolve, other than my pain.

These youth had hoped to rouse the hunter in me
    And transform from tempter to the desired.

But, no. They sought a heart not mine to bestow,
    For it belonged to my creator Mohan –

My personal love-lord Krishna far away,
    Who through separation, I only loved more. [3]

Yet one, a colonel's son amidst my young friends,
    Shone bright from amongst the other jewel-tone boys.

A swain of wealth and poise, his sire led forces
    Of battle flags and elephant battalions.

---

[3] Mohan is one of the soubriquets of Lord Krishna, meaning "Enchanting One," or "Heavenly Lover."

And oh, his lad – were I to describe his looks,
    The appeal of his beauty would require

I say no more in life while my tongue spoke with
    His praise through every breath my mind's wish could draw.

When the dear was drowsy, or when a hand raised
    To halt a nascent yawn, my heart would rise too

And yearn in me to take that hand and give him
    What his lips claimed they wanted from my body.

In short, he was the cup-bearer of men's wants –
    Yielding, loving, and towards me, so gentle.

One day he said to me these words, speaking then
    As if not to disturb the distance tween us:

"I know," murmured he soft, "lovesick dervish have
    No place to call their own, so come home with me.

If you trail me now and be mine, each footfall
    Towards my house I'll sweep with happy teardrops."

Wearied body, and mind, and soul – I followed;
    I moved into his rooms; into his life thus.

For he loved me and grew kinder as if he
  Nursed a poor invalid back to the world's fold.

He'd let no other than himself assist me;
  Claimed he was mine to use as complete servant.

He would bathe me with his own hands at nighttime
  When we soaked in the home's private Turkish bath.

If afterwards, I refused to dine, he too
  Would go hungry, though it pained his young person.

Through all my sleepless nights, he too stayed awake,
  Holding silent vigil, wishing pain away.

To kill the waking hours of day, he would spin
  Me adventures told in storytelling lilts.

Or he'd sing me his songs with poignant passion,
  Inquiring which best suited my morose state.

But no solace would long remain, and fleeting
  As the respite from hurt might have been, my grief

Would nights return stronger than when seen in day,
  Till one moonlit morn, he took my hand, saying:

"Observe the clouds toying frailly in the gloom;
    Let's you and I stroll through the dark garden now.

Perhaps at night," said he, "more clarity shows
    Than all the mind's physic can bring to the light."

So he, my host, fairer than ever before,
    Kept hold my hand tightly as he the way led.

Splendor was all around: peacocks slept 'neath trees,
    Preferring, like men, their own kind to females;

A light mist glazed intrigue upon dull objects,
    Turning mundane into mystique everywhere.

It hung amongst the leaves, and fell from blossoms
    Like scents that rise from sun-loving flowerbeds;

It carpeted walkways and sparkled dearly
    Beneath the stars' all-seeing eyes from above . . .

But these proved no match for the boy beside me
    When we settled upon a marble bench then,

Letting the day's early hours find us still
    Clasping hands together as if lovers true.

Yet when I glanced at his expectant gaze – oh
    – The more perfect he seemed, the less happy I.

His beauty was a sharp despair because it
    Reminded me of my lost man far from here.

Madness, perhaps, to pine, and yet – of you those
    Who've felt as I will understand the sorrow;

Here in fulfillment's pall, I missed my beloved
    Ever more acutely than even before.

Mused I, regarding the round orb overhead,
    "In this, our workaday life, the Lord's presence

Is like the moon gilding the night, for our faith
    In God is like a moth stretching fragile wings

To soar to Luna's height, and ultimately,
    Life's a deception to think we ever can."

When I turned back to him, my sweet young man had
    Allowed a look most skeptical to show through.

"And what of love?" the soldier's son of me asked.
    "It's no bastion of fairytales, dear Dervish;

It is a gift God gives to grant remembrance
    Of where we've sprung, and which we hope to return."

I had to twist away – my fine lad was right,
    And took on some of Luna's greatest appeal.

Patience worn thin, my angel asked yet kinder,
    "Is there nothing here to make you feel tender?

If not for me, then why not for God's bounty –
    Which cradles us softly upon His breezes."

To my reply of *You do not understand,*
    He said, "I may, but start from the beginning."

"Lovely youth," replied I, "I fell victim once
    To one too quick to act upon deception.

"My tale is not unique; perhaps all heartache
    Stems from but one universal estrangement."

"But what," asked he, "his name, place, and time you met?"
    Told I: "The one whose feet the dust I envy

"Was a Brahman scholar, a boy of ten years
    When first he came through my Muslim part of town.

Although a wisp a mere seven years of age,
　　His learnèd bearing spoke to my inmost soul,

For poetry I'd discovered already,
　　And my heart was prepared to receive Love's will.

Alas, seven years were to pass before I
　　Could feel his presence near to me once again.

Seventeen years of age, he returned to speak
　　To crowds gathered upon the steps of our mosque.

And afterwards, I walked up to him shyly,
　　Aware how his beauty was praised by all tongues.

I asked his name, and he seemed taken by
　　The fourteen-year-old who stood coyly near him.

'Why don't you bring your sacred scriptures someday,'
　　I dared suggest, reaching out for both his palms,

'And take them to my house for private study.
　　In exchange, I'll share my books of Persian verse.'

Soon he appeared within my lonely chambers,
　　Where we both fell in love with one another.

Then all our time was spent in each other's glow,
    For he could hardly bear to spend a moment

Separated from me, for when he went home,
    He found he could no longer sleep by himself,

And would return in the middle of the night
    To our matrimonial bed 'neath my roof,

As we one person had become – not two men –
    And no two lovers have thus lived so fully.

We were engulfed in flame any eye could see,
    And gossip, both heartless and kind, reached his folks.

Strict in their Hindu sect, they made threat to cast
    Their boy out on the street as *untouchable.*

Yet when they saw us together, they could tell
    Our union was commanded by the Lord's will.

'This Muslim lad and Brahman scholar,' said they,
    'Are blessed to be bound by eternity's clasp.'

All strife then set aside, a Shah I felt crowned
    By a jewel more noble than a diamond sphere:

I had my Brahman's love, and poetry flowed
   More precious than the lifeblood sustaining two.

But like a snake in the garden citadel,
   An evil one hissed into my lover's thoughts.

And though we'd been content seven lengthy years,
   A tortured lie turned his mind away from me.

A perfidious fool, envious of love,
   Told my true mate I'd been unfaithful to him

And shattered our life as one with jealousy –
   My spouse left our home for his parents' abode.

He abased me in public squares, saying I
   Was the one who had lied, though I never had.

But knowing him better, I understood how
   The deception could be lifted from his sight.

That's why I'd wait for him before his gateway,
   And throw myself into the ground at his feet.

He'd hear no truth the slurs he'd heard when all false,
   Berating me freely once more in the street.

No attempt to remind him of our bond worked,
    For Mind had set his Heart against his beloved.

And now, another seven years afterwards,
    He's still only the one about whom I think.

Since then, a wandering exile I've traveled far,
    Singing my verse for those able to hear me."

As my own tones faded, the garden returned
    To the forethought of boy and dervish alone.

The east was beginning to brim with colors,
    Contrasting sadly with the soldier's son's face.

Wan with his sleeplessness, and for my sorrow,
    I needlessly summed up my heartbroken tale.

"That, dear young man, is how I became quarry
    To faithlessness, and of a broken promise."

Piteous woes now fully relayed, I saw
    My host become disposed more tenderly yet.

"Dervish"—the young man was choking back his tears—
    "Forget that fool, for he's not equal your love.

"Renounce the dupe, because I'm the one here now;
    The one willing to do anything you ask.

Command me think that night is day; or again,
    That light is dark and we should seek but escape;

Or that the soil is but the sky seen wrongly,
    And I will accept what you say is righteous,

For I love you, Dervish, and each man's love is
    To him like an eternity of longing."

Now allowing his tears to flow, his head fell
    On my shoulder in despondency's languor.

How precious this boy was in his truthfulness,
    And how lost as well to belief in my worth.

"How can one," replied I, "fix a broken heart
    With another broken by a heartless one?

Can two damaged and flawed truly heal others?
    For no, two wrongs well-meant can only increase

The acuteness the other feels throughout life,
    And the suffering one must endure for him."

He reached to embrace me, and we stayed locked thus
  Until he fell asleep in my arms sweetly.

Carrying him to bed, I vowed to save him
  Further torment caused by remaining here more.

That afternoon, while the beautiful boy slept –
  With worry exhausted I'd caused him to feel –

I left his house. There was no reason he should
  Suffer from pain my own as much as I do.

Alone once more, with none to care about me,
  The weeks and months dragged on as I drifted lost.

Bodily conditions drained me: coldness crept
  To watch hunger and thirst be my companions.

My thoughts grew blurred; my will, a thing to puzzle;
  And yet, onward I limped, too earth-bound to fade.

The lack of sustenance nursed me on anguish,
  Supping me on heartache's bitter saltiness,

And exiled me to my ravings completely,
  For every cypress tree I saw, I'd embrace,

Finding my belovèd's features calling me
　　Like his limbs were the tree's, and the tree's, like his.

Wary soon of people, whose pity turned rank,
　　And spoke of locking me away, out of sight,

I kept alone and aloof from the roadways
　　Where travelers often stopped to talk to me.

Into the fields I went, feeble and starving –
　　Sunburnt by day, and shivering 'neath the stars.

At last, the time came to seek out a bower
　　Where like an injured bird, I could hide myself.

Therefore, I sought to perish me on the wastes
　　Of the Thar Desert's sands, to shrivel away.

My clothes turned to rags there; my songs stopped trickling;
　　The locusts pitied me and flew on their way,

Knowing no mouthful of meat I'd provide them
　　In my desiccated, once humanly form.

Forty days of torment I withstood before
　　I resolved to claw me up Mount Abu's slopes.

I felt compelled to learn one thing 'fore I died,
    And though the way was hard, I continued on.

Over gravel, amid boulders, through gullies,
    My bloodied fingers pulled me up to the heights.

With the last ounce of strength at my weak command,
    I rose slow into a kneeling position.

"Why?" I cried unto Him from the summit's peak –
    So pale, so exhausted before my God's works.

"Did you create me merely to feel sorrow?
    Were all moments of joy prelude to dolor?

Help me, O Lord, to understand the reason
    I've felt so close to all, yet more removed from

Everything that ordinary people use
    As balm to soothe the setbacks of existence—"

My breath grew shorter then as I struggled hard
    To lift eyes to the heavyset vault of sky.

"So why, merciful One, make me suffer thus –
    Alone, ever seeking meaning from my pain?"

And then, hazy waves of starlight murmured soft
    In visual mirage around my being.

Peering towards the ground beneath my kneeling,
    I watched the mountain dirt transform into stone –

Into the cobbles before my lover's gate
    With stillness all around and the air grown sweet.

My heart, near bursting in my chest, questioned not
    This sudden return to where my partner lived.

Then through the gate's radiant glow, he appeared:
    My beloved in all his beauty, and smiling.

Although I felt the life exiting my frame,
    No greater reward might I have dreamed about.

He came to my side and, gently as a thought,
    Assisted me to rise to my feet once more.

Embraced, he then whispered into my sore ears,
    "How long have I waited for you to come back.

All I've done was to show you, my belovèd,
    How I suffer for those who truly love me.

Now come"—he took my hand—"and I will lead you
   Into the walled garden that is my abode,

For I have set a place for you at supper,
   And our ecstasy shall be for all of time."

Though weak, and hobbled yet by life's anxiousness,
   I took faltering steps toward my new home,

For thus, I followed my Lord God, rejoicing
   That this world's love *is* prelude for what's to come.

Endnotes

---

[i] For an introduction to the scope of Gay writers/poets working in various metaphysical schools of thought throughout time, but where each author praised the nobility of same-sex love as superior to cross-sex sexual relations, see *The Essential Gay Mystics* [Andrew Harvey, Editor] (Edison, New Jersey, 1997)

https://archive.org/details/ess
entialgaymyst0000unse

[ii] The title of Siraj's poem makes for an excellent case study. Although *Bustan-e-Khayal* is a mere three words in length, the term "garden" fails to properly encase the Persian concept of one, which in Farsi is بوستان [bustan], or a walled citadel enclosing a green oasis for reflection and contemplation – like the gardens of the Taj Mahal. And indeed, this brings with it shades of another Persian term for a walled garden: فردوس [firdous, which shares the same root as the English term "paradise"]. Additionally, beginning in the 19th century, *bustan* was also applied to open-air parks, without walls, in city centers. There had been no such things as "public parks" before this date in time.

> Khayal is altogether a more difficult term to parse. As a noun, it carries strong metaphysical meanings of the orphic, revelatory, divination, the hidden, the esoteric, the mystical; plus, ecstasy, quietism, holiness, and the enchanting. In more mundane contexts, *khayal* can be used to speak of a parable, fairytales, or storytelling – i.e., a fiction, but one with the built-in intent to teach a moral lesson.

[iii] *"Siraj Aurangabadi: The Garden of Delusion* [sic] *(Urdu)"* by Saleem Kidwai in *Same-Sex Love in India: Readings from Literature and History* [Ruth Vanita / Saleem Kidwai, Editors] (Kundli, India, 2020), ps. 169-172. Kidwai tells us the original poem contains 1,162 couplets.

[iv] The website Rekhta.org hosts several online retrospective editions of Siraj Aurangabadi's work, all of which contain *Bustan-e-Khayal.* See here:

https://www.rekhta.org/author
s/siraj-aurangabadi/ebooks/